The Country Flowers of a Victorian Lady

The Book

of

Memory

O, like a Book of Sport thou'lt read me o'er!
But there's more in me than thou'lt
understand.

ESSE QUAM VIDERE

The Country Flowers of a Victorian Lady

Fanny Robinson

Introduction and commentary by

Gill Saunders
Curator, Department of Prints, Drawings and Paintings
Victoria and Albert Museum, London

HarperCollins*Publishers*

Originally published in Great Britain in 1999 by Apollo Publishing Ltd, 17 Langbourne Mansions, Highgate, London N6 6PR.

FIRST U.S. EDITION

Designed by David Fordham

Library of Congress Cataloging-in-Publication Data has been applied for.

ISBN 0-06-019703-X

00 01 02 03 04   10 9 8 7 6 5 4 3 2 1

Contents

Introduction

*T*HE BOOK OF MEMORY, reproduced here in its entirety, is a delightful discovery. A handmade keepsake or gift, it is self-evidently a labour of love, created over a number of years by an amateur artist, Fanny Robinson (1802-1872), later Mrs William Hubbard Burrell. We do not know precisely when she began the sequence of paintings that make up the book, though she was certainly at work on it in her forties. Nor do we know for whom the book was made. The poetical extracts are somewhat ambiguous, and it is never entirely clear whether the "you" addressed is a lover or a friend, a man or a woman. It was rumoured in her family that the book was dedicated to someone who had died in a hunting accident – perhaps a student at Magdalen College, Oxford, which is pictured in the border of Plate 19. The poetry is often nostalgic, and many of the flowers illustrated symbolize sentiments such as Submission to Grief, Consolation, Early Friendship and Pleasing Remembrances. Indeed the title, "The Book of Memory", seems to confirm that we should see this charming work as a very personal memorial to a loved one, and a meditation on love and friendship. We can never fully know its creator's intentions; as the title page rightly says, "But there's more in me than thou'lt understand."

This exquisite album of paintings is essentially a naturalist's collection of flower studies, each designed to resemble a page from a medieval illuminated manuscript, with decorated borders and elaborated capital letters.

Although Fanny was an amateur, she was obviously talented and skilful. Of course, sketching and painting in watercolour were standard to a middle-class girl's education in her time, and the art of illumination was also considered an appropriately genteel pursuit for women. Botany, too, was seen as an "amusement for the ladies", and many popular guides to wildflowers and garden plants were written by, and for, women.

Giving gifts of flowers is a long-established custom that we continue enthusiastically today. We give flowers and potted plants for birthdays, at Christmas and on anniversaries of all kinds. A bunch of flowers can be a token of love, a way of saying sorry, or a message of congratulations for any achievement, from passing a driving test to having a baby. But although we use flowers on many occasions to convey particular sentiments, the meanings we attach to specific flowers are sadly limited compared to the complex and subtle Language of Flowers available to the Victorians. Only the faintest echoes of this language are to be found now

6

in our choice of flowers and plants: red roses are still "ambassadors of love" (and as such they command a high price around Valentine's Day), but no one now associates red chrysanthemums with the same emotion. White lilies still carry connotations of innocence and purity, but they are also funeral flowers, and thus have uncomfortable associations with death. Generally speaking, the traces of plant-related superstition that survive in our present-day beliefs and customs have more in common with medieval folklore and religious symbolism than with the minutely codified Language of Flowers developed in the nineteenth century.

Symbolic meanings have always been attached to flowers in religion, heraldry, painting and literature, and in daily life, arising from their use as culinary herbs or medicines. Certain flowers have held traditional meanings for centuries; for example, the iris and the lily both appear in early paintings of the Virgin Mary, as emblems of her purity. Other associations have been drawn from the stories and characters of Greek mythology. The meanings attached to the narcissus (Egotism) and hyacinth (Sorrow) are taken directly from their mythological roles. This mixture of folklore, herbalism, Biblical references and myths has been drawn upon by many writers, including Shakespeare. He made meaningful references to flowers and herbs in most of his plays, and some of these associations were later adopted by the authors of the various Languages of Flowers (for example, rosemary as symbolic of remembrance).

So there was a rich tradition of attaching symbolic meanings to plants available to the writers of the various books that attempted to set out a systematic Language of Flowers. The earliest of these books were French and were published, often anonymously, in the first decades of the nineteenth century. Perhaps the most influential of these was *Le Langage des Fleurs* (Paris 1818) by "Charlotte de la Tour". This was a pseudonym for Louise Cortambert, wife of the geographer Eugène Cortambert. An English translation of this book appeared in 1834, and was hugely successful. In the tenth French edition, published in the 1850s, La Tour claimed, with some justification, that this system of attributing symbolic meanings to flowers had achieved an extraordinary popularity in England. Several English writers published their own versions of the system: the Reverend Robert Tyas, author of several popular botany books for children, published *The Sentiment of Flowers; or, Language of Flora* in 1842, and *The Handbook of the Language and Sentiment of Flowers* three years later (together with other titles on the same theme throughout the 1850s and 1860s). Thomas Miller wrote *The Poetical Language of Flowers*, which appeared in 1847; and Anna Christian Burke published an *Illustrated Language of Flowers* in 1856.

In these books the writers assigned concepts, qualities or emotions to many hundreds of flowers, as well as grasses, herbs, trees, and even fruit. Using these lexicons of plant lore, a carefully chosen bouquet could be put together to convey a complex message. The sender could pursue a courtship or reject a suitor, convey feelings of admiration and friendship, or express unhappiness or disappointment. Every subtle shade of emotion could be communicated by the precise combination of flowers, leaves and fruits.

Beyond the choice of the flowers themselves, there were other subtle clues that could be used to amplify or elaborate upon the message. A bouquet tied with a ribbon to the left indicated that the flowers were intended to say something about the sender; if tied to the right, the meaning applied to the recipient. In addition, a flower or stem might be included in the bouquet, but upside down, implying that the usual meaning of that flower should be inverted. So, a twig of hawthorn, which would normally represent Hope, would be taken to mean Despair if turned upside down. The meaning could be complicated further by stripping away leaves or thorns. Tyas gives the example of a rosebud. Stripped of its thorns, it says "there is everything to hope for"; stripped of its leaves, it says "there is everything to fear". He also explains that when a flower was worn in the hair, or as a corsage or buttonhole, subtle shades of meaning could be inferred from its position and even from the direction in which it leaned.

Fanny Robinson was clearly familiar with the Language of Flowers when she created her "Book of Memory", and by putting together a sequence of painted flowers she was able to tell a detailed visual story, the themes of which are reflected in the accompanying lines of verse. An advantage of creating bouquets in paint instead of out of living flowers was that Fanny was able to put together plants and fruits from different seasons. For example, in Plate 3 she shows the spring-flowering primrose growing with the summer-fruiting strawberry. However, it is not always easy to interpret the meanings of the plants and flowers in Fanny's watercolours. Unfortunately, we do not know which of the many published versions of the Language of Flowers she had read. And the authors of these works did not always agree on the meanings of the flowers, the mock orange (*Philadelphus coronarius*, Plate 9) being a good example. For some it is an emblem of Fraternal Affection (or brotherly love), but other writers take it to mean Counterfeit (or fake), a confusion about meaning that arises because the various authors were themselves using different sources. For the mock orange, Robert Tyas (and his main source, de la Tour) drew on the story of Philadelphus, one of the Ptolemies, the kings of Egypt, whose name means Brotherly Love. Other English authors preferred to attribute to plants meanings that were based on their common English names (rather than their

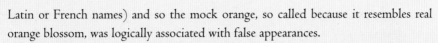

Latin or French names) and so the mock orange, so called because it resembles real orange blossom, was logically associated with false appearances.

Many of the meanings ascribed to flowers in the English publications are surprising, and seem to have no plausible connection with the plant's name or its appearance or history. But the explanation for this lies in the fact that most of the authors were using the French system as their source, so were working from the French common name rather than the English. For example, motherwort (*Leonurus cardiaca*) is usually given the meaning Secret Love, which only makes sense in relation to the French name, which translates as Clandestine. The prudish English writers also tended to modify the more ardent or explicit French meanings: de la Tour gives the meaning *"enivrement"*, that is, Intoxication or Ecstasy, to the heliotrope; in English books this was generally softened to Devotion. English writers also deviated from the French in other ways. For example, where a plant's symbolic meaning was already well established in English literature this meaning was generally preferred. One writer, Thomas Miller, tried to counteract the French influence in the Language of Flowers by compiling a list of meanings based on floral metaphors he found in the work of English poets. However, the French system was too popular for Miller's efforts to have much real influence.

The Language of Flowers was not simply a medium of personal communication. In literature it was often woven into the plot, giving the reader clues to unspoken feelings. Edith Wharton's *The Age of Innocence* (published in 1920, but set in the 1880s) employs flower motifs to reveal the contrasting emotions felt by the protagonist, Newland Archer, towards his fiancée, May, and her exotic married cousin, the Countess Olenska. To May he sends a daily bunch of lilies-of-the-valley; these modest, sweet, self-effacing flowers symbolize the Return of Happiness (see Plate 19). But to Ellen Olenska he sends "some rather gorgeous yellow roses", flowers that signify either Decrease of Love or Infidelity. Ellen has already left her husband, and yellow roses are an ironic presentiment of Archer's subsequent adulterous passion for her.

With the passage of time, this Victorian Language of Flowers has fallen into disuse, and the true significance of Fanny's charming book is likely to remain a mystery. Nevertheless, we can continue to enjoy her delightful and accomplished flower studies, the tender sentiments, and the pleasures of speculation.

GILL SAUNDERS
Department of Prints, Drawings and Paintings
Victoria & Albert Museum, London

Thoughts, that have tarried in my mind,
and peopled its inner chambers,
The sober children of reason,
or desultory train of fancy,
The fruits I have gathered of **memory**
the ripened harvest of my musings,
These give I unto thee.

PLATE I

Pansies & Forget-Me-Nots

Viola spp., Myosotis sylvatica

The sweet forget-me-nots
That grow for happy lovers.
The Brook, TENNYSON

THE PANSY and the forget-me-not are among the most familiar symbols in the Language of Flowers. In both cases the name of the plant is synonymous with its emblematic meaning. Pansies take their name from French, in which they are known as *pensées*, meaning thoughts. This association had become commonplace by the sixteenth century: in Shakespeare's *Hamlet* the deranged Ophelia runs through a litany of flowers and herbs with symbolic meanings that would have been familiar to many in the audience. She begins, "There's rosemary, that's for remembrance; pray, love, remember: and there is pansies, that's for thoughts."

The symbolism of the forget-me-not is self-evident, but the name seems to have come into English usage quite late. It was popularized by Coleridge in his poem *The Keepsake* (1802), inspired by a German folktale, in which the flower is both love token and memento. In the context of the poem it seems that the plant referred to was the water forget-me-not (*Myosotis scorpioides*), but the name became associated with others of the same species. Taken together with the verse below, the flowers illustrated in this plate suggest that Fanny is addressing a lost or absent lover and making a subtle but poignant declaration that she will be true to the memory of their love.

Thoughts that have tarried in my mind,
and peopled its inner chambers,
The sober children of reason,
or desultory train of fancy,
The fruits I have gathered of memory,
the ripened harvest of my musings,
These give I unto thee.

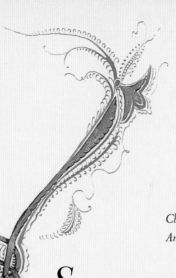

PLATE 2

Snowdrops

Galanthus nivalis

Chaste snowdrop, venturous harbinger of spring,
And pensive monitor of fleeting years!
                    To a Snowdrop, WORDSWORTH

SNOWDROPS have been favourites in English gardens since Elizabethan times. As they are among the few plants that flower in winter, it is hardly surprising that they have come to represent Hope. For some authors, notably Robert Tyas, they also mean Consolation because they seem to promise that spring is coming and offer us a consoling pleasure towards the end of winter. Indeed, one of the alternative names for the snowdrop is "snow piercer". Fanny has dated this page "Jan XIX", so it must have flowered early that year.

The verse describes a solitary snowdrop languishing in a cottage garden, with its head drooping despondently. But the poet also declares that this modest, delicate flower is far more beautiful than anything grown in the artificial warmth of a greenhouse or conservatory.

It was a Bud beside a cottage door
That hung its head in dying languishment
Pensively drooping, nor in glass roof'd store
Are blossom'd aught so fair.

It was a Bud beside a cottage door
That hung its head in dying languishment
Pensively drooping, nor in glass roof'd store
Are blossom'd aught so fair,

Jan XIX

PLATE 3

Primrose & Wild Strawberry

Primula vulgaris, Fragaria vesca

Ring-ting! I wish I were a Primrose,
A bright yellow Primrose, blowing in the Spring!
Wishing, WILLIAM ALLINGHAM

IN THE ILLUMINATED LETTER "O" Fanny has painted a miniature view of Cheddar Gorge (in Somerset). The poetry refers to the "merry days when we were young" and thus may suggest that Fanny had once visited the gorge in the company of the person for whom "The Book of Memory" was created. The flowers she has chosen for this page are associated with fond reminiscence and happiness. Most writers on the Language of Flowers agreed that the primrose, traditionally a symbol of Spring, represents Early Youth. Its common name comes from the medieval Latin *prima rosa*, the "first rose" of the year.

The strawberry is given the emblematic meaning of Perfect Goodness. In some books the strawberry blossoms themselves have the additional meaning of Foresight. This association between the strawberry and ideas of goodness probably arises from the delicate flavour of the fruit; the berries of the wild plant are much smaller than the cultivated strawberry we eat today, but also much sweeter. One of the many kinds of wild food to be found on a country walk, they were often picked and eaten by children, and it may be that Fanny's memories included such childhood pleasures.

O the merry days when we were young,
By hill and forest glen,
We chased the shadows then,
None could be
Blithe as we,
In the merry days when we were young.

O the merry days when we were young,

By hill and forest glen,

We chased the shadows then,

None could be

Blithe as we,

In the merry days when we were young.

Jan^{ry} IXth

I saw a little band pass by —
The flush of youth was on their brow,
Its carols on their tongue,
And sounds of jocund merriment
Upon the breeze were flung,
And one I marked of all the rest,
In life and spirits gay,
With cheek all bloom, and eye all bright,
Speed on his joyous way.
Again — a tramp of horse — I mark
The self-same band pass by;
Upon each brow a darkened gloom;
A tear within each eye.
But where is he, that gallant youth?
Why stands his steed alone?
Woe's me! he was, and he is not —
Into that chasm thrown!
Upon that morning gay has set,
An eve of sorrow, and regret.

Augst XIIth

PLATE 4

*T*HE BOOK OF MEMORY was designed to look like an illuminated manuscript, probably a Book of Hours. The art of illumination, like sketching and painting in watercolours, was seen as an appropriately genteel pursuit to which ladies might devote their leisure time and their creative energies. It was also thought to be more spiritually rewarding than other feminine crafts, such as embroidery or crochet-work. A variety of instruction manuals were published from the 1840s onwards and it seems likely that Fanny had studied some of these books, or had perhaps taken tuition from a specialist drawing master. The scrolling foliage, the decorated capital letters and the layout of the page are all similar to those in original medieval manuscripts, although not consistently of any one style or period.

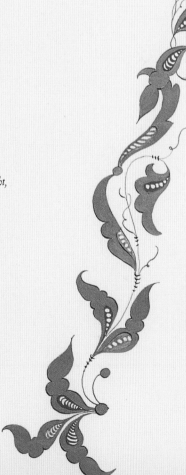

I saw a little band pass by -
The flush of youth was on their brow,
Its carols on their tongue,
And sounds of jocund merriment
Upon the breeze were flung,
And one I marked of all the rest,
In life and spirits gay,
With cheek all bloom, and eye all bright,
Speed on his joyous way.
Again - a tramp of horse - I mark
The self-same band pass by;
Upon each brow a darkened gloom;
A tear within each eye.
But where is he, that gallant youth?
Why stands his steed alone?
Woe's me! he was, and he is not -
Into that chasm thrown!
Upon that morning gay has set,
An eve of sorrow, and regret.

PLATE 5

Flowering Quince, Apple Blossom & Daffodil

Chaenomeles speciosa, Malus spp., Narcissus spp.

And then my heart with pleasure fills,
And dances with the daffodils.
        I Wandered Lonely as a Cloud, WORDSWORTH

RICHLY DECORATED in blue and gold, this plate is an impressive example of Fanny's skill in the art of illumination. As can be seen, she delighted in the practice of embellishing a text with Gothic-style lettering and scrolling flowers and foliage, in the manner of medieval manuscripts.

Here, her flower study unites a daffodil with a branch of flowering quince and a sprig of apple blossom. The quince is a decorative spring-flowering shrub, in Anna Christian Burke's writings said to represent Temptation. Traditionally, of course, the apple tree represented Temptation, because the fruit that Eve gave to Adam was generally referred to as an apple. However, in the Language of Flowers apple blossom is used to express Preference and, as in Plate 11, the daffodil symbolizes Regard. Only Henry Phillips, whose attributions were often eccentric, gave an alternative meaning for the daffodil; for him, it represented Deceitful Hope.

Taken together, we might see this odd group of flowers as an expression of Fanny's romantic preference for someone admired, but perhaps unavailable.

Life's path
To the affectionate and thankful heart
Can never prove a desert. By its side
Fresh springs gush freely forth from time to time
As old ones are dried up, or left behind
In our swift pilgrimage.

Life's path

To the affectionate and thankful heart
Can never prove a desert. By its side
Fresh springs gush freely forth from time to time
As old ones are dried up, or left behind
In our swift pilgrimage.

PLATE 6

Honeysuckle

Lonicera periclymenum

Y'ave heard them sweetly sing,
And seen them in a round;
Each Virgin, like a spring,
With honey-suckles crown'd.

Marmion, Canto III, SCOTT

HONEYSUCKLE is one of those flowers that has several meanings ascribed to it. Most contemporary writers on flower symbolism, including Robert Tyas, said that it symbolized the Bonds of Love. This seems very apt, since honeysuckle is a climbing plant that entwines itself around its support; in the wild it often grows through and over a hedge. As a garden plant it was popular for arbours and could create a secret, shady bower in which courting couples could enjoy a few moments of privacy. In Shakespeare's *A Midsummer Night's Dream* honeysuckle (or woodbine, one of its other names) grows on Oberon's bank – "quite over-canopied with luscious woodbine" – and Titania tells Bottom that she will "wind thee in my arms … So doth the woodbine the sweet honeysuckle gently entwist."

It would seem that Fanny Robinson found the scent of the honeysuckle particularly evocative; the verse suggests that its sweet fragrance, rather than the modest flowers, attracts attention.

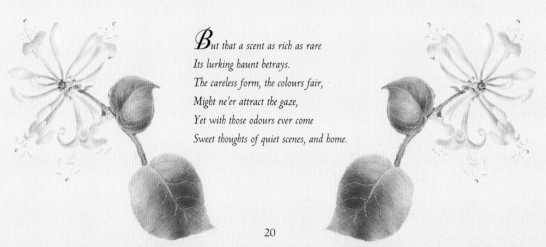

But that a scent as rich as rare
Its lurking haunt betrays.
The careless form, the colours fair,
Might ne'er attract the gaze,
Yet with those odours ever come
Sweet thoughts of quiet scenes, and home.

But that a scent as rich as rare
Its lurking haunt betrays,
The careless form, the colours fair,
Might ne'er attract the gaze;
Yet with those odours ever come
Sweet thoughts of quiet scenes, and home.

But when thy Roses came to me,
My sense with their deliciousness was spell'd;
Soft voices had they _ that, with tender plea,
Whispered of peace, and truth, and constancy unquell'd.

PLATE 7

Moss Rosebuds & Mignonette

Rosa spp., Reseda odorata

The flower of sweetest smell is shy and lowly.
Miscellaneous Sonnets, WORDSWORTH

MOSS ROSES ARE "sports" or mutations of normal roses, the name moss coming from the soft fur-like spines that grow from the surface of the sepals. In the nineteenth century hundreds of moss hybrids were bred from a single centifolia moss rose. The writer Robert Tyas, following Charlotte de la Tour, gave two meanings — Love and Voluptuousness — to the moss rose. Anna Christian Burke preferred a more restrained interpretation: according to her, moss rosebuds made a confession of love.

It was generally agreed that the unassuming flowers of the mignonette conveyed the message "Your qualities surpass your charms", so the flower's meaning was derived directly from the physical character of the plant. Although the flowers are small and nondescript, they give off a delicious scent. In other words, its essential but intangible virtues exceed its physical charms.

But when thy Roses came to me,
My sense with their deliciousness was spell'd;
Soft voices had they - that, with tender plea,
Whispered of peace, and truth, and constancy unequall'd.

PLATE 8

Daisy

Bellis perennis

Wee, modest, crimson-tippèd flow'r . . .
To a Mountain Daisy, BURNS

THE DAISY IS ONE of the most common and familiar of all wildflowers. Its name is a modification of "day's eye", as befits a flower that opens with the dawn, and the pinkish tint to the underside of the petals is like a reflection of the rosy skies at sunrise. For Shelley, the daisy was "The constellated flower that never sets", and many other poets and writers have compared the profusion of daisies scattered in the grass to constellations of stars. Indeed, it is an image that recurs in the verse here.

In the Victorian Language of Flowers it was generally agreed that the daisy was a symbol of Innocence. As the writer Robert Tyas said, it is a child's flower. Daisies are abundant and easy to find, and are often used in children's rhymes and games. Most of us know the simple pleasure to be had from making daisy chains: slitting the stem of one flower with a fingernail, then threading the next stem through the hole, and so on. Fanny's simple, unpretentious picture precisely captures the daisy's modest appeal.

The daisy stars, earth's constellations be;
These grew so lowly I was forced to kneel;
Therefore I pluckt no Daisies but for thee.

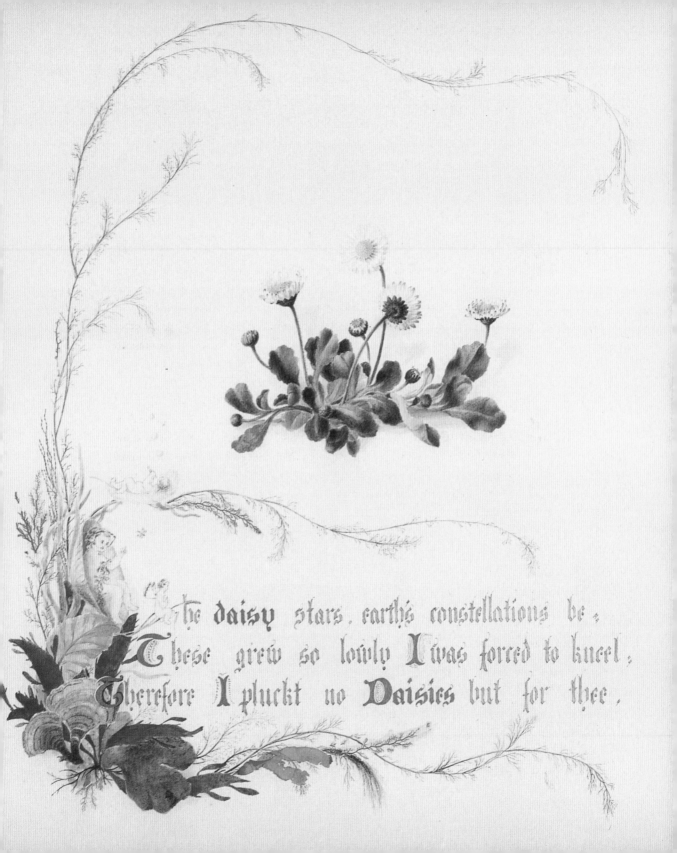

The daisy stars, earth's constellations be,
These grew so lowly I was forced to kneel,
Therefore I pluckt no Daisies but for thee.

I've lived to hear your wedding Bells,
That sound my last fond hope dispels.
I stood unseen within that church,
I saw you pause within the porch,
Then saw you kneeling by his side
When one more happy claim'd his Bride.

PLATE 9

Mock Orange & Rosebuds

Philadelphus coronarius, Rosa spp.

Gather ye rosebuds while ye may,
Old Time is still a-flying:
And this same flower that smiles to-day,
To-morrow will be dying.
   To the Virgins, to Make Much of Time, HERRICK

*T*HIS IS ONE of the most intriguing pages in the book. The illuminated verse seems to address a woman, apparently a love-rival, with the "hope" dispelled being Fanny's hope of marriage to the groom or, less literally, a man whose love she cannot win.

The flowers' meanings are also ambiguous. The philadelphus is commonly known as mock orange, but the various authorities on the Language of Flowers disagreed about the plant's emblematic meaning. Robert Tyas, whose books drew heavily on myth and history for their interpretations, believed the philadelphus to represent Fraternal Affection, or brotherly love. He explained this by referring to the story of Philadelphus, one of the Ptolemies, kings of Egypt, who showed great love for his brother and so became associated with this virtue. By contrast, Anna Christian Burke used the flower's common name, mock orange, and therefore took it to mean Counterfeit, or Fake. This is apt because the mock orange is named for its resemblance to real orange blossom, a symbol of Fertility traditionally carried by a bride. A rosebud generally represented a young girl, and the wedding imagery of this plate is reinforced by the white ribbon tied around the stems and the capital "I", in the form of a church pillar.

I've lived to hear your wedding Bells,
That sound my last fond hope dispels.
I stood unseen within that church,
I saw you pause within the porch,
Then saw you kneeling by his side
When one more happy claim'd his Bride.

I dearly love sweet relics brought
From spots where I have been
They seem to certify the facts
Of Memory's pictured scene.

PLATE 10

Roses & Fuchsia

Rosa spp., Fuchsia spp.

Flowers worthy of paradise.
Paradise Lost, MILTON

*H*ERE A PRETTY, PALE ROSE sets off an extravagant spray of fuchsia flowers. The accompanying verse suggests that these flowers are intended to serve as keepsakes, souvenirs of the past and reminders of former happiness. Fanny's implication is that it was her habit to gather flowers from the places she visited, and this may explain the sometimes unlikely combinations of images that occur in "The Book of Memory".

The oval sketch of a view across a lake or beside a shore may be a keepsake of a fondly remembered place to which the verse alludes. The location has not been identified, but since most of the other vignettes in "The Book of Memory" seem to be drawn from life, it is likely that this one, too, is of somewhere that Fanny had visited.

I dearly love sweet relics brought
from spots where I have been
They seem to certify the facts
Of Memory's pictured scene.

29

PLATE II

Daffodils, Primroses, Dog Rose, Hawthorn & Periwinkle

Narcissus spp., Primula vulgaris, Rosa canina, Crataegus monogyna, Vinca major

Fair daffodils, we weep to see
You haste away so soon:
As yet the early-rising sun
Has not attained his noon.

To Daffodils, HERRICK

THIS DELIGHTFUL BOUQUET of spring flowers expresses Friendship, Regard and Hope – but the poetry is more melancholy, suggesting that emotions, like flowers, fade and are forgotten. An idyllic coastal landscape appears within the capital "P", as if seen through a window on the past. The poetry refers to several flowers – hawthorn, eglantine (honeysuckle) and lilies – although only the first appears in the picture. Fanny has painted a deep-pink variety of hawthorn, not the more common white-flowered May. The hawthorn is known as the May-tree after the month in which it flowers, and as a flower of spring and early summer it generally symbolizes Hope. Traditionally, however, the hawthorn has been the focus of superstition, and to this day some people believe that taking the blossom into a house will bring bad luck, even a death.

Also included in this bouquet are primroses, emblematic of Early Youth, periwinkles, suggesting Early Friendship, dog roses, which represent Pleasure and Pain, and daffodils to convey Regard. Interestingly, the accompanying poetry closely echoes the fifth verse of Keats's *Ode to a Nightingale*.

Pink Hawthorn and the pastoral Eglantine
Fast fading Lilies and broad spreading Leaves
Fair May's bright garland,
But lovely things are fleeting - Spring's sweet flow'rs
Are fugitive - and swifter still than these
Will love dissolve into forgetfulness.

Pink Hawthorn and the pastoral Eglantine

Fast fading Lilies and broad spreading Leaves

Fair May's bright garland,

But lovely things are fleeting—Spring's sweet flow'rs

Are fugitive— and swifter still than these

Will love dissolve into forgetfulness,

PLATE 12

Rhododendrons

Rhododendron spp.

And in the woods a fragrance rare
Of wild azaleas fills the air,
And richly tangled overhead
We see their blossoms sweet and red.
      Spring Scatters Far and Wide, DORA READ GOODALE

R HODODENDRONS AND AZALEAS (see Plate 29), were introduced into British gardens in the early decades of the nineteenth century. As the poetry suggests, they are woodland shrubs, with brightly coloured flowers, mostly in shades of pink and purple. Though they are commonplace now, at that time they were considered rare and exotic. Anna Christian Burke was one of the few writers to attribute a meaning to the rhododendron; she said it was a signal of Danger, conveying the warning to "Beware".

This is one of Fanny's most elegant compositions, beautifully finished with the capital "W" elaborated into a fanciful arcade of Moorish arches. A group of figures can just be made out in the soft verdant landscape beyond.

W hen breezes are soft, and skies are fair,
I steal away from study and care,
To revel awhile in the woodland, where
The flowers are bright, and rich, and rare,
And fresh the breath of summer air.

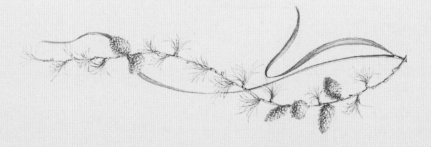

hen breezes are soft, and skies are fair,
I steal away from study and care,
To revel awhile in the woodland, where
The flowers are bright, and rich, and rare,
And fresh the breath of the summer air.

Feb ry vi

PLATE 13

Camellias

Camellia japonica

The faintest streak that on a petal lies
May speak instruction to initiate eyes.
The Mystery of Flowers, BRYANT

THIS BEAUTIFUL STUDY of red and white camellias is one of Fanny's most accomplished watercolours. The flowers are framed within an ornamental border in the style of a medieval illuminated manuscript, and within the decorative flourishes at the lower-right corner "February VI" has been inscribed. Presumably this is the date on which Fanny painted this page, though it may have some other significance – perhaps a birthday or anniversary of some kind. Details such as this are scattered throughout the book, tantalising clues whose true significance may only be guessed at.

One Victorian ascribes a distinctly negative meaning to the camellia, which at that time was also known as the Japan Rose. Henry Phillips, in his *Floral Emblems* (1839) said that the camellia conveyed the message "Beauty is your only attraction" because it had beautiful flowers but no scent. Robert Tyas did not include the camellia in *The Sentiment of Flowers* (1842), but in other contemporary writings the red flower represented Loveliness and the white Excellence. Fanny may have intended that these qualities be associated with herself or with the recipient of the book. However, both can equally be seen as characteristics of "The Book of Memory".

PLATE 14

Roses

Rosa spp.

And I will make thee beds of roses,
And a thousand fragrant posies.

The Passionate Shepherd to His Love, Marlowe

Roses and rosebuds appear a number of times in "The Book of Memory", but this is the only plate devoted to the rose alone. Appropriately, the central bouquet is framed by lightly sketched rose leaves and twining, thorny stems. The rose is one of the oldest cultivated plants and is also the national flower of England. In the Victorian Language of Flowers many varieties and colours of rose are distinguished, each being given a slightly different meaning. Nevertheless, for most writers on the subject "the rose belongs to Venus", goddess of love, and was therefore associated with Love and Beauty, just as it is today.

It is difficult to make a precise identification of the roses that Fanny has included in this charmingly informal group, but they appear to include wild roses – the dog rose (*Rosa canina*) – and the deep-pink *Rosa gallica*. The dog rose also features in Plate 11 and is generally thought to represent the idea of Pleasure and Pain. This meaning might easily be attributed to the majority of roses, which combine lovely blooms with sharp thorns, and has obvious parallels with love itself, where hurt and disappointment can coexist with a deep attachment.

Ye speak of hope, and love,
Bright as your hues, and vague as your perfume;
Of changeful fragile thoughts -
Of sudden fading - midst the tempest's strife
As fall your petals fair.

Ye speak of hope, and love,
Bright as your hues, and vague as your perfume;
Of changeful fragile thoughts—
Of sudden fading—midst the tempest's strife
As fall your petals fair.

.... Laburnum rich

In streaming gold, Syringa ivory pure,

And Lilac, various in array.

PLATE 15

Lilac, Laburnum & Mock Orange

Syringa vulgaris, Laburnum anagyroides, Philadelphus coronarius

O were my Love yon lilac fair,
Wi' purple blossoms to the spring,
And I a bird to shelter there,
When wearied on my little wing
BURNS

*T*HIS IS ONE OF THE FEW illustrations to which a purely descriptive verse is attached (with each of the flowers mentioned by name). However, Fanny has called the white flowers syringa, the name often mistakenly used for the mock orange. Perhaps she did so because she intended it to represent Memory. (*For a fuller account of the meanings ascribed to the mock orange, see Plate 9.*)

Just as the flowers themselves are harmoniously grouped, so the emotions and sensations they represent complement and illuminate each other. All the authorities on the Language of Flowers agree that the purple lilac expresses the First Emotions of Love. As Robert Tyas explained, the lilac's chief beauty lies in its flowers with their rich, heady scent, but these are short-lived and transient, like the first intense pangs of love.

The golden flowers of the laburnum hang down in cascades, giving it a melancholy, "weeping" appearance. Perhaps for this reason, most writers defined its meaning as Forsaken, or alternatively Pensive Beauty. The addition of "syringa", meaning Memory, suggests that these emotions belong to the past.

*L*aburnum rich
In streaming gold. Syringa ivory pure,
And Lilac, various in array.

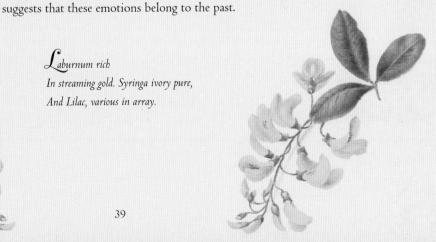

PLATE 16

Scarlet Geranium, Gentian, Heliotrope, Canary Creeper, Wild Oats, Ferns & Grasses

Pelargonium spp., Gentian spp., Heliotropium spp., Tropaeolum peregrinum, Avena fatua

Geranium boasts
Her crimson honours, and the spangled beau,
Ficoides, glitters bright the winter long.

COWPER

A PUZZLING RANGE of emotions is suggested by the various elements of this elegantly composed bouquet. For the writer Robert Tyas, the scarlet geranium was an emblem of Folly, though in other sources it was said to represent Stupidity or given the meaning Comforting. The delicate mauve flowers of the heliotrope were thought to express Devotion, while the bright blue gentian declares "You are unjust". Fern fronds represent Fascination, but grasses were used to represent Utility or Usefulness. Wild oats appear to have no specific attribution in the Language of Flowers, but the "sowing of wild oats" has long been a metaphor for youthful promiscuity.

This plate features one of the most detailed and charming of the book's illuminated initials. The scene shows a ladies' archery contest, and the border is decorated with straps and tassels, quivers and arrows – perhaps a subtle reference to Cupid's arrows of love. The initials R.C.B. are minutely inscribed on a flag, and a ribbon below carries the Latin motto *Fortis fortuna adjuvat* ("Fortune favours the bold"). Sadly, R.C.B. has not been identified, and we cannot know whether Fanny was claiming boldness for herself or urging it on another.

Lose not this morn delicious - the blue sky
Is clear, and woos thee forth so lovingly,
Leaf, blade, and tiniest daisy-bud grow bright
In the reflection of the golden light,
Come.

ose not this morn delicious — the blue sky
Is clear, and woos thee forth so lovingly,
Leaf, blade, and tiniest daisy-bud grow bright
In the reflection of the golden light,
Come

PLATE 17

Star of Bethlehem, Flowering Currant, Polyanthus & Dog's-Tooth Violet

Ornithogalum umbellatum, Ribes sanguineum, Primula x polyantha, Erythronium dens-canis

April showers bring forth May flowers.
ENGLISH PROVERB

USING THE LANGUAGE OF FLOWERS, a subtle and complex message could be composed by putting together a bouquet of mixed blossoms, either of living plants or, as here, of painted ones. Unfortunately for later generations unversed in this arcane language, the code often resists a full translation.

Here Fanny Robinson illustrates the seasonal reference of the couplet below with a nosegay of spring-flowering plants. The delicate white-flowered star of Bethlehem symbolized Purity, and the showy polyanthus was, somewhat surprisingly, said to represent Diffidence. But the meaning of the flowering currant remains obscure, and the dog's-tooth violet (so named for the shape of its root) has an ambiguous role: as a violet it would connote Modesty, but it is in fact a species of lily, and as such would share the attributes of the star of Bethlehem. It is possible that Fanny meant to represent herself by these feminine and self-effacing virtues. She drew on familiar associations and on contemporary codifications of flower symbolism, together with more obscure references, to forge a deeply personal language of love, loss and reminiscence.

Spring returns, the flowerets blow
Will hope return? ah no.

Spring returns, the Flowerets blow
Will Hope return? oh no

And Indian plants of form and hue
The richest that ever were fed on dew.

PLATE 18

Orchid Cactus

Epiphyllum ackermanii

Earth laughs in flowers.
Hamatreya, EMERSON

MANY PLANTS were newly introduced to Europe in the nineteenth century, yet these exotics were rarely attributed any significance in the Language of Flowers. The cactus was mentioned by some authors, but none of them recognized the separate species. As a genus the cactus was given a rather straightforward meaning, being said to represent Warmth, an obvious reference to its origins in hotter, sunnier lands. The poetry betrays how little Fanny knew about the plant she has depicted — in fact it came from Mexico, not from India. She makes a further misleading reference to its exotic origins by including a sketchy drawing of what appears to be a date palm, below which a turbaned figure is seated.

And Indian plants of form and hue
The richest that ever were fed on dew.

PLATE 19

Bluebells & Lily-of-the-Valley

Endymion nonscriptus, Convallaria majalis

Shaded Hyacinth, always Sapphire Queen of the mid-may.
KEATS (of the bluebell)

THE BLUEBELL is generally agreed to signify Constancy, but various meanings have been attributed to the lily-of-the-valley. For some it symbolized Humility; alternatively it was also held to represent the Return of Happiness. It certainly had longstanding associations with the Virgin Mary, arising out of its later identification with the "lily of the valleys" in the Song of Solomon. In German folklore, it was said to have sprung up from the tears the Virgin shed at the foot of the cross.

The bluebells' association with constancy may derive from the character of the plants themselves, with their extraordinary resilience: they can survive the greediest gatherings of their flowers, provided that the leaves are not trampled down. The sight of a wood carpeted with bluebells can be magical and has often inspired poets to hyperbole. Tennyson memorably likened bluebells to the sky breaking through the earth.

Where are my thoughts?
Where full on dome, and tow'r and spire.
Sunset is glowing;
And slow through meadows green, inlaid
With flowery grove, and poplar glade,
Isis is flowing.

Where are my thoughts?
Where full on dome, and tow'r, and spire,
Sunset is glowing;
And slow through meadows green, inlaid
With flowery grove, and poplar glade,
Isis is flowing.

May vm.

I take
Sweet flowers fresh and fine,
With pleasant thoughts I bind them,
And greetings intertwine.

PLATE 20

Pelargoniums & Nasturtiums

Pelargonium spp., Tropaeolum majus

So from the root
Springs lighter the green stalk, from thence the leaves
More aerie, last the bright cunsummate flower.

Paradise Lost, MILTON

*T*HIS PRETTY POSY of garden flowers seems not to carry a specific message. As the verse says, gifts of flowers express "pleasant thoughts" and "greetings". Robert Tyas wrote that a bouquet of flowers could simply represent Gallantry or Politeness, just as it does today when sent as a "Thank you" or presented to the hostess of a party. Certainly the meanings of these flowers have no obvious relevance to the general themes of "The Book of Memory". The pelargoniums, more commonly called geraniums, were said by some writers to represent Eagerness, and nasturtiums generally stood for Patriotism. Both were favourite garden plants in the nineteenth century, pelargoniums being especially popular in the 1830s and 1840s, when many different varieties were grown, either as summer bedding plants or as pot plants.

*I*take
Sweet flowers fresh and fine,
With pleasant thoughts I bind them,
And greetings intertwine.

PLATE 21

Greater Stitchwort, Marsh Marigold & Germander Speedwell

Stellaria holostea, Caltha palustris, Veronica chamaedrys

To create a little flower is the labour of ages.
Proverbs of Hell, WILLIAM BLAKE

THIS PRETTY BUNCH of wildflowers has the simple charm of a child's gift. The kingcup, or marsh marigold, is one of Britain's most ancient flowering plants and for centuries was an important harbinger of spring. It was considered a powerful plant, effective against evil influences. Hung upside down in doorways on May Day, it was supposed to ward off witches; and the sun-like golden flowers were used as a protection against lightning. Some of this folklore significance may have persuaded Fanny to include it here, because the marsh marigold did not appear in any contemporary books on the Language of Flowers. Nor indeed did the stitchwort, a pretty, common flower of the wayside and woodland.

Of the three, only the speedwell was mentioned in books of floral emblems. It was said to represent Fidelity, though some authors gave it the more precise meaning of Female Fidelity. There is no obvious reason for this attribution. Traditionally the speedwell was worn by travellers as a good-luck charm against accident or delay; indeed, it gets its common name from the fact that speedwells are roadside plants, and their bright "eyes" were thought to speed the traveller on his way.

And he called the flowers, so blue and golden,
Stars, that in earth's firmament do shine.

And he called the flowers, so blue and golden,
Stars, that in earth's firmament do shine.

The swelling downs where sweet air stirs
Blue harebells lightly, and where prickly furze
Buds lavish gold. ✦━━✦━━✦━━✦━━✦━━✦

PLATE 22

Harebells & Gorse

Campanula rotundifolia, Ulex europaeus

I love the gorse and heather,
And hare-bells close beside —
I'll find my cap and feather,
And kiss a Highland bride!
   The Rose is a Royal Lady, C. G. BLANDEN

*T*HROUGHOUT THE BOOK, Fanny's wide-ranging knowledge of indigenous plants and flowers is evident both in the poetry and in the paintings, and it is likely that she observed her subjects on country walks and in her garden. Most of the watercolours are finely drawn and give enough detail of the plants' structures to allow precise botanical identifications, which suggests that she was an enthusiastic amateur botanist, as were many middle-class women of the time. Here the poetic extract is a quotation from Keats's poem *Endymion*, which correctly locates harebell and gorse as plants of the downland (dry, open grassland).

According to the writer Anna Christian Burke, the harebell symbolized Submission to Grief, but gorse (which Fanny calls by its alternative common name, furze) is another of those plants that seem not to have had any specific meaning in the Victorian Language of Flowers.

In a characteristically charming detail, Fanny depicts a mushroom as the capital "T" of Keats's verse.

*T*he swelling downs where sweet air stirs
Blue harebells lightly, and where prickly furze
Buds lavish gold.

PLATE 23

Rosebuds & Forget-Me-Nots

Rosa spp., Myosotis sylvatica

The sweet forget-me-nots
That grow for happy lovers.
The Brook, TENNYSON

THERE ARE MANY VARIETIES of rose, and many different colours, and each was given a slightly different meaning in the Victorian Language of Flowers. For Robert Tyas, rosebuds were symbolic of young girls, and there was of course ample literary precedent for this: poets often used the rosebud as a metaphor for youthful beauty or for transience, because the rosebud represents a moment that is short-lived. Robert Herrick expresses this in his poem *To the Virgins, to Make Much of Time*, when he says "Gather ye rosebuds while ye may."

Like the rosebuds, forget-me-nots appear several times in Fanny's "Book of Memory". They represent True Love, and get their name from a German legend in which a young man dies in the act of picking some of these flowers for his sweetheart. Falling, fatally, into the river beside which they were growing, he throws the flowers at her feet with the parting words "Forget me not!". Here, however, the poetry seems to refer to an absent friend, not a lover. Taken together, the flowers and the verse suggest that Fanny is recalling a youthful friendship.

Friendship's offering,
Whose silent eloquence, more rich than words,
Tells of the giver's faith, and truth, in absence,
And says "Forget-me-not".

Friendship's offering,
Whose silent eloquence, more rich than words,
Tells of the giver's faith, and truth, in absence,
And says "Forget-me-not".

PLATE 24

Sweet Peas

Lathyrus odoratus

Here are sweet peas, on tiptoe for a flight:
With wings of gentle flush o'er delicate white,
And taper fingers catching at all things,
To bind them all about with tiny rings.
        I Stood Tip-toe Upon a Little Hill, KEATS

*H*ERE THE ILLUMINATED LINES of verse make an apt comparison between the delicate pinks and purples of sweet peas and the colours of sunset-tinted clouds. These are flowers that share the softness and transparency of watercolour.

The sweet pea has been a favourite summer garden plant since the sixteenth century. It is a relative of the edible pea but probably acquired the name "sweet" pea in recognition of its delicious scent. As cut flowers sweet peas look best massed together, as shown here in Fanny's painting, gathered into a bouquet that includes the full range of colours. Once cut, however, the sweet pea fades quickly, and the various symbolic meanings that have been ascribed to it relate to its fragile, ephemeral character. In the Victorian Language of Flowers some writers suggested its meaning as Departure, although for Anna Christian Burke it symbolized Delicate Pleasures.

*D*elicate pink,
Purple, and snowy white are on thy wings
Fair Butterfly of Flowers: Thy many tints
Are dyed as if the sunset evening clouds
Had fallen to the earth in sudden rain
And left their colours.

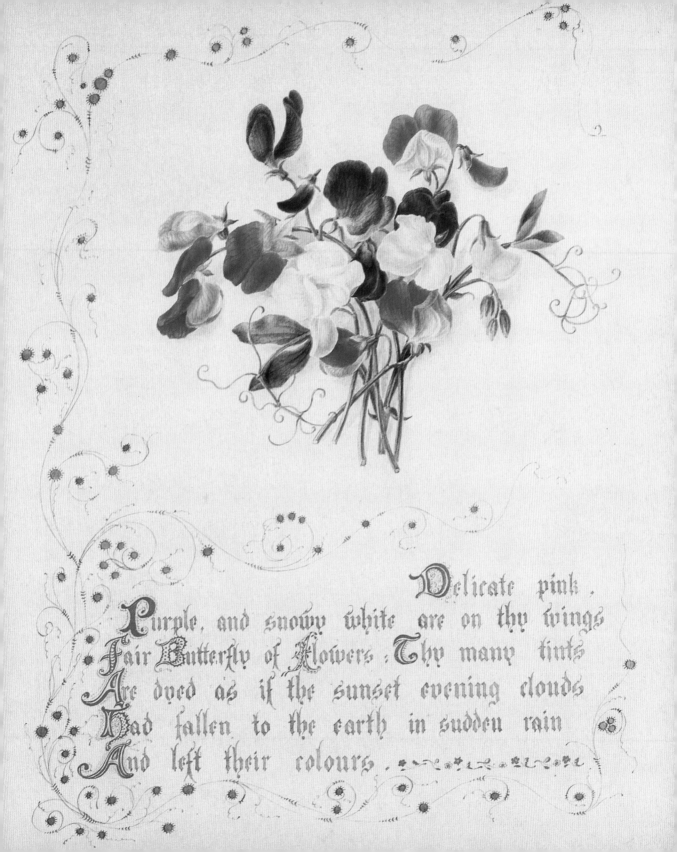

Delicate pink,
Purple, and snowy white are on thy wings
Fair Butterfly of Flowers, Thy many tints
Are dyed as if the sunset evening clouds
Had fallen to the earth in sudden rain
And left their colours.

The Misletoe hung in the Barons Halls,
And the Holly-bush brightened the old oak walls.

Sing heigh ho! the Holly!

PLATE 25

Holly, Mistletoe & Christmas Rose

Ilex aquifolium, Viscum album, Helleborus niger

The Holly and the ivy,
When they are both full grown,
Of all the trees that are in the wood,
The holly bears the crown.

TRADITIONAL CAROL

THESE THREE PLANTS all have long-established associations with Christmas. To emphasize this, Fanny has added details such as a church spire framed by ringing bells, and festive revelry in a grand medieval hall (presumably the "Barons Halls" of the verse). Holly and mistletoe are traditionally brought into the house as decoration at Christmas. Both evergreens, they were believed to have magical protective properties at this dead time of year, and to represent nature's powers of regeneration. Most of the folklore surrounding holly and mistletoe has pagan origins, but holly was also incorporated in Christian customs because it was said to symbolize Christ's crown of thorns. Mistletoe, however, retains its pagan associations as an emblem of fertility, and the custom of kissing under the mistletoe continues as a faint echo of earlier beliefs.

In the Language of Flowers holly represented Forethought. Robert Tyas suggested that this was because holly grows spiny leaves to protect itself from grazing animals. To Victorian commentators mistletoe – which generally grows on the highest branches of trees – meant "I surmount difficulties" or "I rise above all"; and, according to Anna Christian Burke, the Christmas rose asks the recipient to "Relieve my anxiety". But none of these meanings seems especially relevant here, the lines of verse – the first two adapted from Thomas Haynes Bayly's *The Mistletoe Bough*, the third the refrain from a song in Shakespeare's *As You Like It* – being purely festive in tone.

The Mistletoe hung in the Barons Halls,
And the Holly-bush brightened the old oak walls.
Sing heigh ho! the Holly!

PLATE 26

Primula, Crocuses & Hepatica

Primula spp., Crocus vernus, Hepatica spp.

I wonder if the sap is stirring yet,
If wintry birds are dreaming of a mate,
If frozen snowdrops feel as yet the sun
And crocus fires are kindling one by one
CHRISTINA ROSSETTI

THIS IS A DELIGHTFUL spring bouquet, as cheerful and full of hope as our first sight of the flowers themselves each year. Many Victorian writers regarded the crocus as being emblematic of the Pleasures of Hope; and some, including Anna Christian Burke, offered the further meaning of Youthful Gladness.

The pretty pastel pinks and blues of the hepaticas make a declaration of Confidence. In explanation, Robert Tyas said that when the flowers appear it is a sign to the gardener that the climate is mild enough for him to sow his seeds with confidence.

The verse celebrates the sweet charms of the flowers illustrated in this plate, which are presented to the reader with the simple informality of a child's gift.

Simple flowers although ye be,
Ye are dearly loved by me;
Simple children - ye no less
Touch me with your lowliness.
Emblems meet
Of all things innocent, and sweet.

Simple flowers although ye be,
Ye are dearly loved by me;
Simple children – ye no less
Touch me with your lowliness.
Emblems meet
Of all things innocent, and sweet.

Then the pied wind-flowers
And Narcissi, fairest of them all,
Who gaze on their eyes in the stream's recess,
Till they die of their own dear loveliness.

PLATE 27

Narcissi, Anemones & Auriculas

Narcissus spp., Anemone spp., Primula auricula

What first inspired a bard of old to sing
Narcissus pining o'er the untainted spring?
…on the bank a lonely flower he spied,
A meek and forlorn flower, with naught of pride,
Drooping its beauty o'er the watery clearness,
To woo its own sad image into nearness:
I Stood Tip-toe Upon a Little Hill, KEATS

ANEMONES ARE NAMED after Anemos, the Greek god of the winds, because the Ancient Greeks believed that the flowers opened only when the wind blew. It is in recognition of this story that they are often called windflowers. However, the most common meaning of the anemone in the Victorian Language of Flowers is Forsaken, which seems also to derive from another Greek myth — when Venus was weeping in the forest for Adonis, anemones sprang from the ground where her tears fell.

The narcissus was named after yet another character in Greek mythology, a handsome shepherd boy who fell in love with his own reflection in a pool and drowned trying to catch this elusive spirit. Thus the flower became a symbol of Egotism, or Selfishness.

The pretty auricula, a flower favoured by Victorian gardeners, conveys the message "Entreat me not".

Then the pied wind flowers
And Narcissi, fairest of them all,
Who gaze on their eyes in the stream's recess,
Till they die of their own dear loveliness.

PLATE 28

Sweet Violet

Viola odorata

Not a flower
But shows some touch, in freckle, streak or stain,
Of his unrivall'd pencil.

The Task, COWPER

THE SWEET VIOLET is so-called on account of its pleasingly seductive perfume, because of which it is sometimes said to be the flower of Aphrodite, the Greek goddess of love. It was a favourite garden plant in medieval times, and writers often commented on its scent. In the sixteenth century, Sir Francis Bacon wrote in his essay *Of Gardens*: "That which above all yields the sweetest smell in the air is the Violet."

This is one of the most charming images in the book. A beautifully observed study of the whole plant, it is drawn with a careful attention to detail (although, strangely, both double and single forms of flower appear to be growing from the same root). Modesty is the virtue most commonly associated with the violet, and this meaning fits well with the character of the plant itself: it is small, grows close to the ground, and prefers shaded spots in woods and hedgerows. The violet also represents Hidden Virtue and Beauty, and – in Christian terms – Humility. Fanny's Christian faith is celebrated by the poetry. The verse suggests that God attends to the intricacies of our thoughts and emotions just as assiduously as to the detail in a violet.

There's not a tender thought, nor sigh,
In the gentlest of meek hearts,
But He who op'd the violet's eye,
And moulded its fair symmetry
Well knows — and balm imparts.

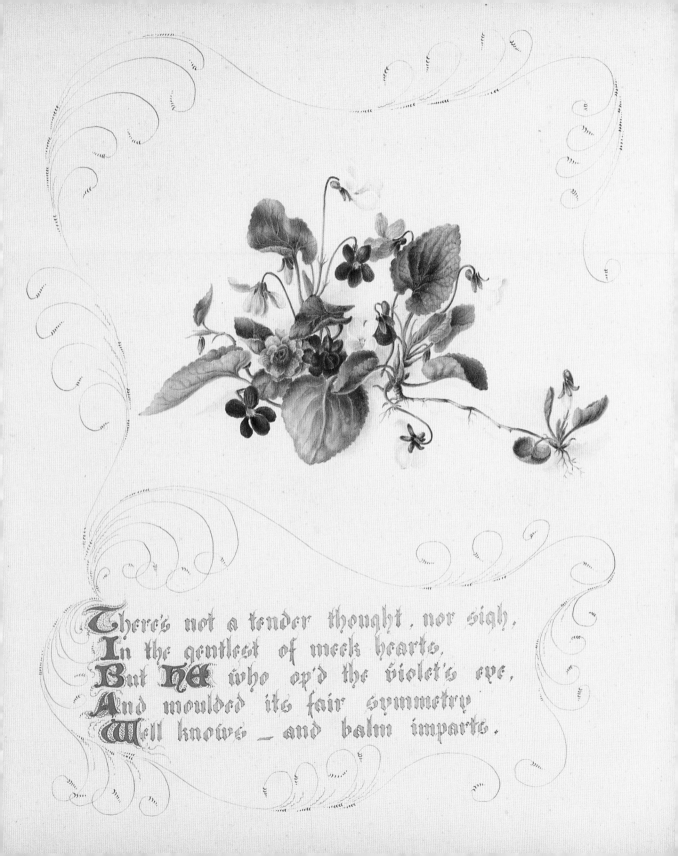

There's not a tender thought, nor sigh,
In the gentlest of meek hearts,
But HE who op'd the violet's eye,
And moulded its fair symmetry
Well knows _ and balm imparts.

She too is blest whose outward eye
The graceful lines of art may trace,
Till out of dust, her magic raise,
A home for prayer and love, and full harmonious praise

Oct 1st

PLATE 29

Azaleas

Azalea spp.

The fair azalea bows
Beneath its snowy crest.
She Blooms No More, SARAH H. WHITMAN

IN THIS PARTICULARLY LOVELY illustration Fanny has grouped together several varieties of azalea in almost every colour. Like rhododendrons (Plate 12), azaleas were first grown in Britain in the early nineteenth century, and in the Language of Flowers these voluptuous blooms were considered, somewhat inappropriately, to represent Temperance. The writer Henry Phillips gave a rather unconvincing explanation for this. He suggested that azaleas flourish in Britain only when planted in "poor, heathy ground"; in rich soil they sicken and die, disappointing the hopes of the gardener, and so might be seen as Temperate, or Restrained, in their need for sustenance.

The extravagantly serpentine capital "S" that introduces the verse frames a charming vignette of a country church. This is one of several churches depicted by Fanny in the illuminated initial capitals of "The Book of Memory". Specific architectural details imply that these are real places, not fanciful inventions.

She too is blest whose outward eye
The graceful lines of art may trace;
Till out of dust, her magic raise,
A home for prayer and love, and full harmonious praise.

PLATE 30

Penstemon, Pansy, Canterbury Bells, Fuchsia & Yew

Penstemon spp., Viola spp., Campanula medium, Fuchsia spp., Taxus baccata

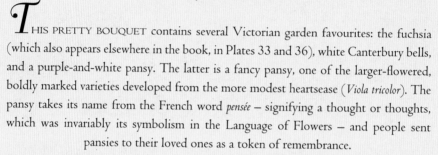

This little purple pansy brings
Thoughts of the sweetest, saddest things.
Heartsease, MARY E. BRADLEY

*T*HIS PRETTY BOUQUET contains several Victorian garden favourites: the fuchsia (which also appears elsewhere in the book, in Plates 33 and 36), white Canterbury bells, and a purple-and-white pansy. The latter is a fancy pansy, one of the larger-flowered, boldly marked varieties developed from the more modest heartsease (*Viola tricolor*). The pansy takes its name from the French word *pensée* – signifying a thought or thoughts, which was invariably its symbolism in the Language of Flowers – and people sent pansies to their loved ones as a token of remembrance.

The campanula, with its spike of white bells, was said to represent Gratitude. Tucked in behind the flowers is a sprig of red-berried yew. Traditionally a churchyard tree, the dark, evergreen yew was an emblem of sadness and sorrow.

Here, as so often in "The Book of Memory", Fanny's choice and combination of flowers suggests that she is invoking tender but wistful memories of the past.

*I*have here only a nosegay of culled
Flowers and have brought nothing
Of my own, but the string that ties them.

I have here only a nosegay of culled **flowers**, and have brought nothing of my own, but the string that ties them.

There's a bower of Roses by Bendemeer's stream
And the nightingale sings there all the day long.

PLATE 31

Red & White Roses, with Bindweed

Rosa spp., Calystegia sepium

Then will I raise aloft the milk-white rose,
With whose sweet smell the air shall be perfumed.
Henry VI, Part 2, SHAKESPEARE

ROSES HAVE ALWAYS BEEN the emblems and ambassadors of love, but Victorian writers on the Language of Flowers differentiated between the many colours and varieties, and gave specific meanings to each. The red rose was the quintessential symbol of Love, just as it is today, while the white rose represented Spiritual Love and Purity.

The fragile flowers of the bindweed (also known as convolvulus because of its twisting, convoluted stems) stood for Uncertainty. Perhaps Fanny was intending to suggest her own uncertainty about the nature of love — but like many of the messages in "The Book of Memory", this is expressed with such subtlety as to be open to many interpretations.

The page is completed with a pretty vignette of a country church that nestles within the sweeping curves of the capital "T".

There's a bower of Roses by Bendemeer's stream
And the nightingale sings there all the day long.

PLATE 32

Water Lilies

Nymphaea alba

Flowers have an expression of countenance as much as men or animals. Some seem to smile; some have a sad expression; some are pensive and diffident; others again are plain, honest and upright...

Star Papers: A Discourse of Flowers,
HENRY WARD BEECHER

*T*HE WATER LILY is yet another of those plants to which very different meanings were given by the various Victorian authorities on the Language of Flowers. For Anna Christian Burke it symbolized Purity of Heart, but for Robert Tyas it represented Eloquence. The source of this association is Egyptian mythology. Tyas explains that the Ancient Egyptians dedicated the water lily to the sun, the god of Eloquence, because the lily flower closes at sunset and sinks under the surface of the water, then rises and opens again at dawn. There is no clue here as to which meaning Fanny Robinson had in mind, but in the context of the book as a whole both are appropriate. Purity, modesty and truth are virtues that occur again and again in her choice of symbolic flowers — and the book itself, combining poetry and paintings, may have been intended as an eloquent address to Fanny Robinson's friend or lover.

PLATE 33

Passionflower & Fuchsias

Passiflora caerulea, Fuchsia spp.

The Amen! of Nature is always a flower.
O. W. HOLMES

*H*ERE THE VERSE focuses on the richly symbolic and spiritual nature of flowers. The references to "holy thought" and the rewards of contemplation are especially appropriate in relation to the passionflower because it has conventionally represented Christian Faith. Indeed, its name refers to Christ's Passion because the structure of the flower is said to resemble all the elements of the crucifixion: a crown of thorns, the scourge, the sponge, the nails and the five wounds of Christ.

The elegant pendant flowers of the fuchsia – three different varieties are illustrated here – were understood to represent Taste. According to Henry Phillips in his *Floral Emblems*, this was because of the "peculiar harmony and beauty" in the "gracefulness" of the flowers. The American passionflower had reached Europe in the seventeenth century, but the fuchsia was not introduced into English gardens until the nineteenth. Robert Tyas, who wrote many books on garden plants, illustrated and described several varieties of fuchsia, and Fanny illustrated a number of "new" plants and exotic species in "The Book of Memory", which suggests that she took a keen interest in gardening.

*T*hus musing in a garden nook
Each flower is as a written book.
And rich the stores of holy thought
That by these blossoms fair are brought.

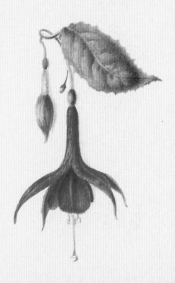

Thus musing in a garden nook
Each Flower is as a written book,
And rich the stores of holy thought
That by these blossoms fair are brought.

Flowers are the gems that children love,
Yet men delight to see,
And they bring a thousand memories
Of by-gone days to me!

PLATE 34

Maidenhair Fern,
Orchid & Monkey Flower

Adiantum capillus-veneris, Orchidaceae, Mimulus spp.

Flowers of all heavens, and lovelier than their names.
The Princess, ALFRED, LORD TENNYSON

*T*HIS PLATE BRINGS TOGETHER some Victorian favourites. Ferns such as the maidenhair enjoyed considerable popularity in the nineteenth century, and were often grown indoors in special glass containers.

Tropical orchids, too, were avidly collected and cultivated. A number of the many female professional botanical illustrators of the period specialized in studies of orchids, among them Miss S. A. Drake and Augusta Withers, "Floral Painter to Queen Adelaide".

Few of these plants have a meaning in the Language of Flowers, which, given their popularity, seems rather surprising. Anna Christian Burke, who compiled perhaps the most comprehensive listing, gave Fascination as the emblematic meaning of the fern, but she did not distinguish between the many different species. Charlotte de la Tour and Robert Tyas were more specific, both asserting that the maidenhair fern represented Discretion. Tyas, as always, gave a rather fanciful explanation for this attribution, saying "this pretty fern conceals from botanists the secret processes in its flowering and seeding", thus embodying the virtues of discretion.

*F*lowers are the gems that children love,
Yet men delight to see,
And they bring a thousand memories
Of by-gone days to me!

PLATE 35

Begonias, Carnation & Periwinkle

Begonia spp., Dianthus caryophyllus, Vinca major

*And because the breath of flowers is far sweeter in the air than in
the land, ... therefore nothing is more fit for that delight than to
know what be the flowers and plants that do best perfume the air.*
Essays: Of Gardens, BACON

THE LINES OF VERSE that accompany this mixed bouquet of garden flowers have no
obvious connection with the flowers themselves, or with the sentiments they represent.
Though they are all summer-flowering plants, none of them is associated with the sea
or with woodland. Of course, this book is a very personal and private creation, and
inevitably some of its meanings are inscrutable to us. However, the general themes
suggested by these flowers are those that run through the book as a whole: memory, past
pleasures and disappointed love.

The blue periwinkle represents Early Friendship and also Pleasing Remembrances – and
yet these happy emotions are overshadowed by Dark Thoughts (represented by the
begonias), and the red carnation is shorthand for "Alas for my poor heart". Thus the
poetry invokes happy times, summer walks and seaside holidays, but the flowers tell a
different story. They suggest that the pleasures of the past, and the youthful friendships,
have been clouded by disappointment and, perhaps, jealousy.

The summer time! the summer time!
The happy idle days!
The wanderings in the shady wood
The sojourns by the sea;
The Sea! Oh what a magic sound
Is that small word to me!

The summer time! the summer time!
The happy idle days!
The wanderings in the shady wood
The sojourns by the sea:
The Sea! Oh, what a magic sound
Is that small word to me!

Delicate as those fair flowers
That blossom but a few short hours,
Yet in that narrow space compress
An age of lavish loveliness.

PLATE 36

Field Bindweed, Fuchsia, Nasturtium, Spiraea & Scarlet Pimpernel

Convolvulus arvensis, Fuchsia spp., Tropaeolum majus, Spiraea spp., Anagallis arvensis

To me the meanest flower that blows can give
Thoughts that do often lie too deep for tears.
    Intimations of Immortality, WORDSWORTH

THIS IS AN UNUSUAL composition for Fanny, being one of the few plates combining wildflowers and cultivated plants. The pale-pink trumpet of the field bindweed and the tiny blossoms of the scarlet pimpernel are pleasingly entwined with showier garden flowers, including the deep-pink pendant blooms of the fuchsia and the orange-gold of the nasturtium.

The message, if there is one, is ambiguous. The convolvulus represents Uncertainty, while the nasturtium stands for Patriotism; the fuchsia (which appears in several other plates) is an emblem of Taste, and the tiny flowers of the pimpernel imply a rendezvous or meeting.

The verse suggests that the flowers pictured here are ones that fade quickly once picked.

Delicate as those fair flowers
That blossom but a few short hours,
Yet in that narrow space compress
An age of lavish loveliness.

PLATE 37

Achimenes & Eccremocarpus

Gesneriaceae, Bignoniaceae

Fresh Spring, the herald of love's mighty king,
In whose coat-armour richly are display'd
All sorts of flowers which on earth do spring
In goodly colours gloriously array'd.

Amoretti, SPENSER

THESE BOLD, EXTRAVAGANT FLOWERS and the elegant variegated leaves belong to species not recognized in the Victorian Language of Flowers. Perhaps Fanny intended that they should simply express gratitude to God for his gift of flowers in all their glorious variety.

Throughout her "Book of Memory" Fanny sometimes depicts familiar plants (to which specific meanings were attributable) alongside more exotic species, many recently introduced to English gardens and therefore excluded from the various dictionaries of the Language of Flowers.

Both the plants pictured here were tender exotics, originally from Mexico and Chile respectively. No doubt their showy opulence made them appealing subjects for Fanny, who was often inspired purely by the aesthetic beauty of her subjects.

Receive
Thanks, blessings, love, for these thy lavish boons
O Thou that giv'st us flowers!

Receive
Thanks, blessings, love, for these thy lavish boons
O Thou that giv'st us flowers!

PLATE 38

Chrysanthemums & Winter Jasmine

Chrysanthemum spp., Jasminum nudiflorum

Out in the lonely woods the jasmine burns
Its fragrant lamps, and turns
Into a royal court with green festoons
The banks of dark lagoons.

Spring, HENRY TIMROD

THREE DIFFERENT COLOURS of chrysanthemum are listed in the nineteenth-century guides to the Language of Flowers, and these are the colours Fanny has illustrated here: red, yellow and white, each of a different variety. The red declares "I love", but the yellow complains of Slighted Love, and the white is an emblem of Truth.

The yellow-flowered winter jasmine stands for Grace and Elegance. Taken together with the lines of verse, it seems that these flowers are offered to cheer and console. This plate is a good example of Fanny's artistic licence in putting together plants that would not flower in the same season. The verse implies that both bloom at the year's end – but chrysanthemums are autumn-flowering, and the scented flowers of the jasmine appear on the bare, leafless branches from midwinter.

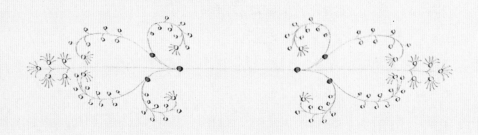

Ye bring your bright blossoms when Summer is gone,
Like new hope, to the heart of a desolate one.

Ye bring your bright blossoms when Summer is gone,
Like new hope, to the heart of a desolate one.

Thus when our Autumn comes, and quietly
We rest contented, but with wings furl'd close,
May we, like it, bind in our garner'd stores
Fresh blooming flowers, nursed into brighter glow
By sunshine of kind looks, and kindly deeds,
While music of kind voices, ever nigh,
Shall be to us, as redbreasts' melody.

PLATE 39

French Marigold, Larkspur, Michaelmas Daisies, Chilean Glory Flower, Asparagus, Hawthorn, Mallow, Rosehips, Cypress, Bellflower

Tagetes patula, Consolida spp., Aster spp., Eccremocarpus scaber, Asparagus officinalis, Crataegus monogyne, Malva spp., Rosa spp., Cupressus spp., Campanula spp.

A MIX OF LATE summer flowers, rosehips and berries makes a vivid bouquet evoking the spirit of autumn. This seasonal theme is carried through in the surrounding motifs, which include emblems of harvest and plenty — ripe ears of wheat and barley, together with grapes, cherries and other fruits.

The meanings implied by this profusion are various and seem to be contradictory. The larkspur represents Lightness or Levity, the mallow stands for Mildness, the hawthorn means Hope, and the bellflower, Gratitude. These positive emotions are offset by the marigold (an emblem of Grief) and the sprig of cypress, which is a traditional symbol of mourning. According to Robert Tyas, when the marigold and cypress are combined, they signify Despair. As so often in "The Book of Memory", Fanny's choice of flowers conveys a complex and highly personal message that is difficult to interpret. The poetry, however, suggests that we may hope that a life of kindness and care will reap a harvest of contentment and security.

Thus when our Autumn comes, and quietly
We rest contented, but with wings furl'd close,
May we, like it, bind in our garner'd stores
Fresh blooming flowers, nursed into brighter glow
By sunshine of kind looks, and kindly deeds,
While music of kind voices, ever nigh,
Shall be to us, as redbreasts' melody.

PLATE 40

Poppies

Papaver spp.

There blossom'd suddenly a magic bed
Of sacred dittany, and poppies red:
At which I wonder'd greatly, knowing well
That but one night had wrought this flowery spell.

Endymion, Book I, KEATS

HERE WE SEE four different varieties of poppy, including two fancy "laced" kinds with their coloured petals edged in white. In the Victorians' Language of Flowers the meaning attributed to the poppy varied according to its colour – the red flower represented Consolation, the white was an emblem of Sleep. This second meaning was traditionally attached specifically to *Papaver somniferum*, the opium poppy, from which opium is extracted.

The poetry guides the reader in the interpretation of this painting. The "furrow'd field" represents the course of life, with all its cares and troubles. The moments of joy in life that console us for unhappiness and loss are therefore like bright poppies enlivening a cornfield. Although Fanny has painted garden varieties of poppy here, she has framed the central posy with a sketched border of cornstalks. These remind us of the field poppy, and thus connect the image and the verse.

Life is like a furrowed field, methinks the Poppies say,
Broadcast sown with care and grief, which spring up day by day,
But ever there, mid crops of care, some bright-hued joy appears,
To teach that men should hope again, for smiles amid their tears.

Life is like a furrow'd field, methinks the Poppies say,
Broadcast sown with care and grief, which spring up day by day,
But ever there, mid crops of care, some bright-hued joy appears,
To teach, that men should hope again, for smiles amid their tears.

rom each carved nook, and fretted bend,
Cornice, and gallery, seem to send
Notes that with seraphs tones might blend.

PLATE 41

Wallflowers

Erysimum cheiri

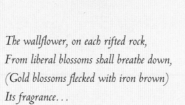

The wallflower, on each rifted rock,
From liberal blossoms shall breathe down,
(Gold blossoms flecked with iron brown)
Its fragrance...
The Birth of Flowers, D. M. MOIR

*T*HIS IS ONE of the prettiest and most accomplished of Fanny's watercolours. The vibrant bouquet is set off by delicately painted organ pipes and a pretty vignette of Ely cathedral (we know that a member of her family lived at "The Cottage", near the cathedral), and the accompanying verse seems to refer to the music of the organ.

According to Robert Tyas, the wallflower's symbolic meaning was Faithful in Adversity. He explained the association by pointing out that it blooms "in places where ruin and desolation prevail" – and, as its name suggests, it does grow readily on old walls and fallen masonry, as well as in cottage gardens.

Fanny's painting shows the flowers set against glossy, green ivy leaves and tied with a trailing tendril. Like the wallflower, ivy is often found growing on ruins and most Victorian authors on the Language of Flowers considered it to be an emblem of Friendship, or of Fidelity and Marriage. Tyas observed that in Ancient Greece a branch of ivy would be presented to a newly wed husband as a symbol of the lifelong union he had just entered into. Indeed, it is ivy's habit to continue growing over its original support – often a tree or a wall – even after the support has fallen. It is, therefore, the perfect metaphor both for Marriage and for Fidelity in Adversity.

*F*rom each carved nook, and fretted bend,
Cornice, and gallery, seem to send
Notes that with seraphs tones might blend.

91

PLATE 42

*T*O EMBELLISH THE PAGES of her book Fanny used a variety of decorative styles adapted from illuminated manuscripts. However, the loops and knots that link and almost obscure the capital letters of each verse on this page are the artist's own fanciful inventions rather than copies of any medieval pattern. Scrolling between the lines of the text are the forms of flowers and leaves in outline. Although they are not of identifiable species, they are nevertheless more naturalistic than the highly stylized loops and knots. In this plate Fanny reiterates the theme of the book – memory – with its power to preserve beauty, love and friendship.

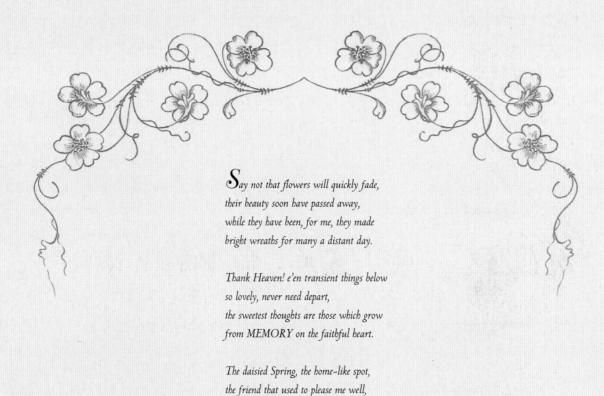

Say not that flowers will quickly fade,
their beauty soon have passed away,
while they have been, for me, they made
bright wreaths for many a distant day.

Thank Heaven! e'en transient things below
so lovely, never need depart,
the sweetest thoughts are those which grow
from MEMORY on the faithful heart.

The daisied Spring, the home-like spot,
the friend that used to please me well,
may pass - but cannot be forgot:-
love's image is indelible!

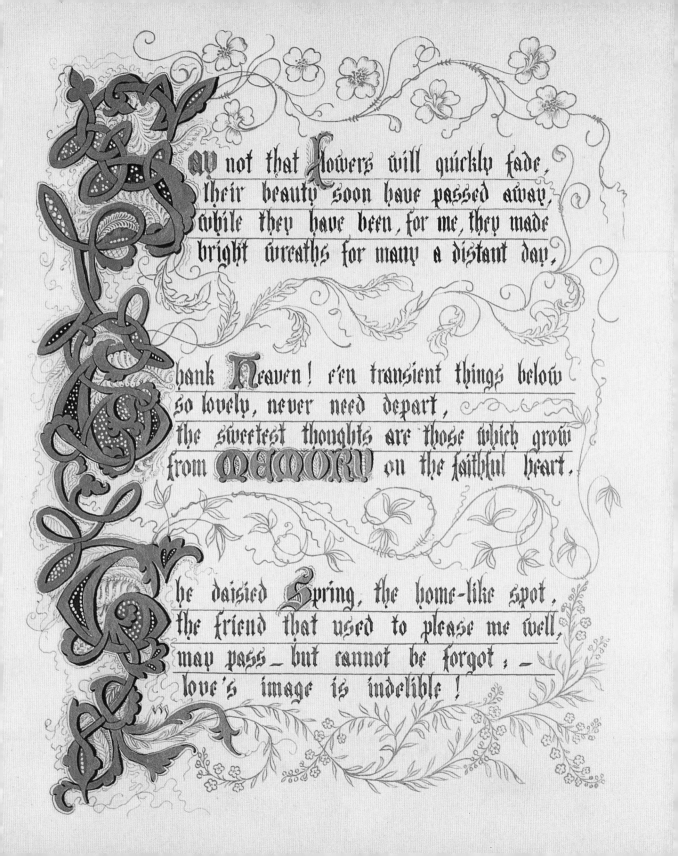

Say not that flowers will quickly fade,
their beauty soon have passed away,
while they have been, for me, they made
bright wreaths for many a distant day,

Thank Heaven! e'en transient things below
so lovely, never need depart,
the sweetest thoughts are those which grow
from MEMORY on the faithful heart.

The daisied Spring, the home-like spot,
the friend that used to please me well,
may pass — but cannot be forgot, —
love's image is indelible!

Index of Flowers

Numerals refer to plate numbers, 'intro' refers to the text of the Introduction.

Bibliography

Burke, Anna Christian [Mrs L. Burke] *The Illustrated Language of Flowers,*
London, 1856 (reissued 1963)
Coats, Alice M. *The Treasury of Flowers,* London, 1975
Goody, Jack *The Culture of Flowers,* Cambridge, 1993
Grigson, Geoffrey *The Englishman's Flora,* London, 1958
Hey, Mrs M. *The Moral of Flowers,* London, 1835
Mabey, Richard *Flora Britannica,* London, 1996
Miller, Thomas *The Poetical Language of Flowers,* London, 1847
Phillips, Henry *Floral Emblems,* London, 1825
Tour, Charlotte de la *The Language of Flowers*
(translated from *Le Langage des Fleurs*), London, 1835
Tyas, Robert *The Sentiment of Flowers; or, Language of Flora,* London, 1842
Tyas, Robert *The Handbook of the Language and Sentiment of Flowers,* London, 1845
Tyas, Robert *The Language of Flowers,* London, 1869

Acknowledgements

Gill Saunders thanks Peter Arris for wordprocessing and additional research.
The publishers are grateful for the kind assistance of Slaney Begley, Patrick Devlin,
Jeremy Gambrill, Dharminder Kang, Julie Kenbrey, Katie Martin-Doyle,
Patricia Mort, Claire Nielson and Pamela Todd.